LET'S STARTED

THE JOURNEY

AI (Artificial intelligence)

*"This **eBook** covers all the essential topics and will help clarify your concepts. It's a valuable resource for preparing for **university / college exams** and **Software Development**"*

- PRANAY BHUTE

ABOUT THE AUTHORS

Pranay Bhute

My name is Pranay Bhute and I have a passion for education and knowledge sharing. I love reading books and writing to help people access information easily. As an educator, I believe in the power of knowledge to transform lives and empower individuals. I strive to make complex topics simple and interesting so that anyone can benefit from them. My goal is to inspire a love of learning and a thirst for knowledge in others. I enjoy connecting with people and helping them achieve their educational goals.

Meet Pranay Bhute, a passionate educator, avid reader, and dedicated author. With a love for both writing and reading, Pranay has made it his mission to share knowledge and inspire others through his words. As an educator, he thrives on helping others learn and grow, making complex topics easy to understand.

"Stay connected! Follow me on

insta – ibhutepranay

linkedIn- ibhutepranay

Acknowledgment Section:

"This book is prepared using guidance and informational support provided by various sources, including OpenAI's assistant."

© 2024 Pranay Bhute. All Rights Reserved.

UNIT -1

General Issues and Overview of AI

- **The AI Problems**

Definition (English):
AI problems are complex challenges that require systems to mimic human intelligence, such as understanding natural language, recognizing patterns, decision-making, and learning from experience.

Features:

- **Unstructured Data Handling:** AI can work with incomplete or ambiguous data.
- **Knowledge Representation:** Storing and manipulating information about the world.
- **Learning and Adaptation:** Improves performance through experience.
- **Problem-Solving:** Finds solutions using heuristic and algorithmic approaches.
- **Automated Reasoning:** Draws logical conclusions from available data.

Advantages:

- **Efficiency:** Solves problems faster than humans in many cases.
- **Accuracy:** Reduces human errors.
- **24/7 Availability:** AI systems do not require rest.
- **Scalability:** Can handle large volumes of data effortlessly.
- **Disadvantages:**

- **High Initial Cost:** Development and deployment can be expensive.
- **Lack of Creativity:** Limited to predefined patterns and algorithms.
- **Dependence on Data:** Requires large and high-quality datasets.
- **Ethical Concerns:** Risk of misuse and bias in decision-making.

In Simple Hindi:
AI problems wo challenges hain jo insani dimaag ke kaam jaise language samajhna, patterns pehchanna, aur decision lena automate karte hain.
- **Khasiyat (Features):**
    - **Data Handle karna:** Incomplete ya confusing data ke sath bhi kaam karte hain.
    - **Learning Ability:** AI systems time ke sath improve karte hain.
    - **Fast Problem-Solving:** Jaldi solutions nikalte hain.
- **Fayde (Advantages):**
    - **Speed aur Accuracy:** Insano ke mukable tezi aur kam galtiyan hoti hain.
    - **Continuous kaam:** Machine bina rukhe kaam kar sakti hai.
- **Nuksan (Disadvantages):**
    - **Costly:** Banane aur chalane me mehnga hota hai.
    - **Creativity ki kami:** Sirf set rules ke andar kaam karta hai.

- ## What is an AI Technique?

- ## Definition (English):
  AI techniques are systematic methods or approaches used to solve AI problems. These include algorithms, search methods, machine learning, and heuristics.

Features:

- **Algorithmic Approaches:** Involves step-by-step problem-solving procedures.
- **Search and Optimization:** Finds the best solution among many possibilities.
- **Heuristics:** Rule-based techniques for quick decision-making.
- **Learning Models:** Uses data to improve performance over time.

Advantages:

- **Improved Efficiency:** Streamlines problem-solving.
- **Adaptability:** Adjusts based on new data.
- **Automation:** Reduces human intervention.

Disadvantages:

- **Complexity:** Requires high computational power.
- **Overfitting Risks:** Models might work well on training data but fail on new data.
- **Interpretability:** Difficult to understand the decision-making process in some cases.

In Simple Hindi:
AI technique ek method hai jo AI problems solve karne ke liye use hoti hai, jaise algorithms aur learning models.

- **Khasiyat (Features):**
    - **Algorithm Use:** Problem solve karne ke liye specific steps follow karta hai.
    - **Learning aur Adaptation:** Nai information ke sath better hota jata hai.
- **Fayde (Advantages):**
    - **Automation:** Human kaam kam ho jata hai.
    - **Improvement:** Naye data ke sath aur achha kaam karta hai.
- **Nuksan (Disadvantages):**
    - **High Power Requirement:** Bahut zyada resources lagte hain.
    - **Complex Understanding:** Har koi easily nahi samajh sakta.

- # Characteristics of AI Applications

- **Definition (English):**
  AI applications exhibit traits like autonomy, adaptability, and interactivity to perform tasks that require human-like intelligence.

Features:

- **Autonomy:** Operates without continuous human guidance.
- **Interactivity:** Communicates and collaborates with users.
- **Adaptability:** Adjusts its behavior based on new data or environment changes.
- **Scalability:** Handles increasing workloads efficiently.

Advantages:

- **Enhanced Decision-Making:** Supports complex analysis for better outcomes.
- **Cost Savings:** Reduces the need for manual labor.
- **Real-Time Functionality:** Processes data and responds immediately.

Disadvantages:

- **Technical Limitations:** May fail in unforeseen scenarios.
- **Dependence on Technology:** Requires stable infrastructure.

In Simple Hindi:
AI applications wo hain jo human intelligence wale tasks automate karte hain, jaise virtual assistants ya self-driving cars.
- **Khasiyat (Features):**

- - **Self-Dependent:** Apne aap kaam karte hain bina bar-bar human help ke.
  - **Adapt karna:** Nai data ke sath apne aap ko update karte hain.
- **Fayde (Advantages):**
  - **Better Decisions:** Complex problems ko analyze karke better result dete hain.
  - **Kam Kharcha:** Manual kaam aur resources kam lagte hain.
- **Nuksan (Disadvantages):**
  - **Technology Dependent:** Stable systems ki zarurat hoti hai.

Introduction to LISP Programming

1. Syntax and Numeric Functions

- **Definition (English):**
  LISP (LISt Processing) is one of the oldest programming languages, primarily used in artificial intelligence research. Its syntax is minimal and relies heavily on the use of parentheses for defining expressions.

Key Features of LISP Syntax:

- **Fully Parenthesized Notation:** Every function and operation is enclosed in parentheses.
  Example: (+ 2 3) for addition.
- **Prefix Notation:** Operators precede their operands.
  Example: (* 4 5) instead of 4 * 5.
- **Numeric Functions in LISP:**
- **Basic Operations:** LISP supports operations like addition, subtraction, multiplication, and division.
  Examples:
    - (+ 2 3) returns 5.
    - (* 6 7) returns 42.
- **Advanced Functions:** Functions for square root (sqrt), exponentiation (expt), and modulus (mod) are also available.

Advantages:

- **Simplified Syntax:** Easy to learn due to minimal syntax rules.
- **Powerful Numeric Operations:** Handles complex mathematical calculations efficiently.
- **Disadvantages:**

- **Verbose Notation:** Heavy use of parentheses can make code less readable.
- **Steep Learning Curve for Beginners:** Prefix notation may be confusing initially.

In Simple Hindi:
LISP ek purani programming language hai jo AI aur data processing me use hoti hai. Iski syntax kaafi simple hai lekin sab kuch parentheses ke andar hota hai.

- **Syntax ki Khasiyat:**
    - Har operation aur function parentheses me likhna padta hai.
    - Operators jaise +, -, pehle aate hain aur baad me numbers.
- **Numeric Functions:**
    - Addition aur multiplication ke liye (+ 2 3) aur (* 4 5) likha jata hai.
    - Complex calculations ke liye sqrt, expt bhi use hota hai.

2. Basic List Manipulation Functions

- **Definition (English):**
  LISP is designed for list processing, and lists are the primary data structure. It provides various functions to create, modify, and manipulate lists.

Common List Functions:

- **car Function:** Returns the first element of a list.
  Example: (car '(1 2 3)) returns 1.
- **cdr Function:** Returns the rest of the list after the first element.
  Example: (cdr '(1 2 3)) returns (2 3).
- **cons Function:** Adds an element to the front of a list.
  Example: (cons 0 '(1 2 3)) returns (0 1 2 3).
- **append Function:** Joins two or more lists.
  Example: (append '(1 2) '(3 4)) returns (1 2 3 4).

Advantages:

- **Dynamic Nature:** Lists in LISP can grow and shrink as needed.
- **Flexibility:** Provides powerful functions for manipulating data structures.

Disadvantages:

- **Performance Overhead:** Operations on large lists can be slow.
- **Complex Syntax for Nested Lists:** Managing deeply nested lists can be challenging.

In Simple Hindi:
LISP me lists kaafi important data structure hoti hain. Lists ke sath kaam karne ke liye kai functions diye gaye hain.

List Functions:
- **car:** List ka first element deta hai.
  Example: (car '(1 2 3)) → 1.
- **cdr:** First element ke baad ka list deta hai.
  Example: (cdr '(1 2 3)) → (2 3).
- **cons:** Ek naye element ko list ke start me add karta hai.
  Example: (cons 0 '(1 2 3)) → (0 1 2 3).

3. Predicates and Conditionals

Definition (English):
Predicates are functions that return a boolean value (true or false) based on a given condition. Conditionals in LISP are used to make decisions based on these predicates.

Common Predicates in LISP:

- **equal or =:** Checks if two values are equal.
  Example: (= 3 3) returns T (true).
- **null:** Checks if a list is empty.
  Example: (null '()) returns T.
- **listp:** Checks if an object is a list.
  Example: (listp '(1 2 3)) returns T.
- **Conditionals in LISP:**
- **if Statement:** Executes a block of code if a condition is true.
  Example: (if (= 2 2) 'yes 'no) returns 'yes'.
- **cond Statement:** Similar to a multi-way if for evaluating multiple conditions.

- **Example:**
  (cond
    ((> 5 3) 'greater)
    ((= 5 3) 'equal)
    (t 'lesser))
  Returns 'greater'.

Advantages:

- **Logical Decision Making:** Helps in making complex decisions within programs.
- **Flexibility:** Offers various ways to check conditions.
- **Disadvantages:**
- **Code Complexity:** Nested conditionals can make code harder to read.

In Simple Hindi:
Predicates wo functions hote hain jo true ya false return karte hain. Conditionals ka use decision-making ke liye hota hai.
- **Common Predicates:**
    - **=:** Dono values ko compare karta hai.
      Example: (= 3 3) → true.
    - **null:** Check karta hai list empty hai ya nahi.
      Example: (null '()) → true.
- **Conditionals:**
    - **if:** Agar condition true hai to ek block execute hota hai.
      Example: (if (= 2 2) 'yes 'no) → 'yes'.
    - **cond:** Multiple conditions ke liye use hota hai.

Input, Output, and Local Variables in LISP

Input and Output (I/O) in LISP

Definition (English):
Input and output operations in LISP handle user input, file handling, and output display.

Common I/O Functions:

- **print:** Displays an expression followed by a newline.
  Example: (print "Hello, World!") outputs: "Hello, World!".
- **write:** Similar to print but without a newline.
  Example: (write "Hello") outputs: "Hello".
- **read:** Reads an input from the user.
  Example: (setq x (read)) stores the user input in x.

File Handling Functions:

- **open:** Opens a file for reading or writing.
- **read-line:** Reads a line from the file.
- **write-line:** Writes a line to the file.

Advantages:

- **Flexibility:** Can handle various input and output operations, including file management.
- **Interactive Programming:** Allows user interaction during program execution.

Disadvantages:

- **Complexity in File Operations:** File handling requires careful management of streams.

In Simple Hindi:
LISP me input aur output ke liye functions diye gaye hain jo user se data lete hain aur result dikhate hain. File handling bhi possible hai.

I/O Functions:

- **print:** Screen par output dikhata hai.
  Example: (print "Hello") screen par "Hello" show karega.
- **read:** User se input leta hai aur variable me store karta hai.

2. Local Variables in LISP

Definition (English):
Local variables in LISP are variables that exist only within a specific function or block of code. They are defined using let or let*.

- **Usage:**
- **let:** Defines local variables and initializes them.

- **Example:**
  (let ((x 5) (y 10))
    (+ x y)) ; Result: 15

let*: Similar to let but allows variables to depend on each other.

- **Example:**
  (let* ((x 5)
         (y (+ x 10)))
    y) ; Result: 15

Advantages:

- **Encapsulation:** Keeps variables local to a function, preventing unintended interference.
- **Efficient Memory Usage:** Variables are discarded after their scope ends.

Disadvantages:

- **Limited Scope:** Variables cannot be accessed outside their defined block.

In Simple Hindi:
Local variables wo hote hain jo ek specific function ya block ke andar hi kaam karte hain. LISP me let aur let* ka use karke inhe define kiya jata hai.

Example:
(let ((x 5))
  (+ x 10)) ; yaha x ki value sirf is block ke liye valid hai.

Iteration and Recursion in LISP

1. Iteration
   - **Definition (English):**
     Iteration involves repeating a set of operations. In LISP, iteration is implemented using loops.
   - **Common Iterative Constructs:**
   - **dotimes:** Repeats a loop a fixed number of times.

     Example:

     (dotimes (i 5)
        (print i))   ; Prints 0 to 4
   - **dolist:** Iterates over each element in a list.

     Example:

     (dolist (x '(1 2 3))
        (print x))   ; Prints 1, 2, 3

Advantages:

- **Efficient for Repetitive Tasks:** Automates repetitive operations.
- **Simple Syntax for Lists:** Easy to iterate over collections.

Disadvantages:

- **Limited Flexibility:** Iterative constructs are less expressive compared to recursion in some cases.
- **In Simple Hindi:**
  Iteration ka matlab hai ek kaam ko baar-baar repeat karna. LISP me loops ke liye dotimes aur dolist ka use hota hai.

2. Recursion

- **Definition (English):**
  Recursion is a process where a function calls itself to solve smaller instances of a problem.

- **Example of Recursion in LISP:**

- **Factorial Function:**

```
(defun factorial (n)
  (if (= n 0)
      1
      (* n (factorial (- n 1)))))  ; Calculates n!
```

Advantages:

- **Elegant Solutions:** Simplifies problems like tree traversal or factorial computation.
- **Powerful for Nested Structures:** Ideal for solving problems with hierarchical data.
- **Disadvantages:**
- **Memory Usage:** Recursion can lead to stack overflow if not handled properly.
- **Performance:** Slower than iteration for some tasks.
- **In Simple Hindi:**
  Recursion ek technique hai jisme ek function apne aap ko call karta hai jab tak problem solve na ho jaye.
  Example: Factorial calculate karne ke liye recursion ka use hota hai.

Property Lists and Arrays in LISP

1. Property Lists
- **Definition (English):**
  Property lists (or plists) are key-value pairs used to store metadata or attributes about an object.

- **Usage:**
- **Defining a Property List:**

  (setq my-plist '(name "John" age 25))

  Accessing Properties:
  Use get to retrieve the value associated with a key.
  Example: (get 'my-plist 'name) → "John".

Advantages:

- **Flexible Data Storage:** Useful for storing related attributes.
- **Dynamic Nature:** Can be modified easily.
- **Disadvantages:**
- **Slower Access:** Property lookup can be slower compared to arrays.

- **In Simple Hindi:**
  Property lists ek key-value pair ka data structure hai. Ye kisi object ke baare me additional information store karte hain.

2. Arrays

- **Definition (English):**
  Arrays are fixed-size, indexed collections of elements, allowing fast access.

  - **Defining an Array:**
    (setq my-array (make-array 5)) ; Creates an array of size 5.

- **Accessing and Modifying Elements:**
- **Access:** (aref my-array 0) retrieves the first element.
- **Modify:** (setf (aref my-array 0) 42) sets the first element to 42.

Advantages:

- **Fast Access:** Indexing provides quick retrieval of elements.
- **Structured Data:** Ideal for tabular data.

Disadvantages:

- **Fixed Size:** Cannot grow dynamically.
- **Less Flexible than Lists:** Operations like insertion/deletion are less efficient.
- **In Simple Hindi:**
  Arrays ek fixed size collection hai jo indexed data ko store karte hain. Inka use fast data access ke liye hota hai.

UNIT-2

Problem Solving in Artificial Intelligence

Definition (English):
1. Problem solving in AI refers to the process of finding a sequence of actions that leads from an initial state to a desired goal state. It involves searching through possible solutions and applying strategies to achieve the objective efficiently.

- **Key Elements of Problem Solving:**

1. **Initial State:** Starting point of the problem.
2. **Goal State:** Desired end condition.
3. **Operators:** Actions or steps to move from one state to another.
4. **State Space:** All possible states reachable from the initial state using operators.
5. **Solution:** Sequence of operators leading to the goal state.

Importance of Problem Solving in AI:

- **Automates Complex Tasks:** Helps machines perform tasks that require decision-making.
- **Optimization:** Finds the best possible solution.
- **Adaptability:** Allows systems to handle new and unforeseen challenges.

In Simple Hindi:
AI me problem solving ka matlab hai ek aise tareeke se kaam karna jisme ek shuruaati halat se le kar antim goal tak pohonchne ka rasta dhoonda jaye. Is process me kai solutions ko explore kiya jata hai aur efficient solution nikala jata hai.

- **Initial State:** Jaha se problem shuru hoti hai.
- **Goal State:** Jaha problem solve ho jati hai.
- **Operators:** Steps ya actions jo ek state se doosri state tak le jaate hain.
- **State Space:** Sabhi possible states ka collection.

- ## Search and Control Strategies

- **Definition (English):**
    - Search strategies are methods used in AI to navigate through the state space to find a solution. Control strategies determine the order in which states are explored.

- **Types of Search Strategies:**

- **Uninformed Search (Blind Search):**
    - **Breadth-First Search (BFS):** Explores all nodes at the current level before moving to the next level.
    - **Depth-First Search (DFS):** Explores as far as possible along a branch before backtracking.

- **Informed Search (Heuristic Search):**
    - **Best-First Search:** Uses a heuristic to evaluate the desirability of nodes.
    - *A Search:* Combines path cost and heuristic to find the optimal solution.

- **Control Strategies:**

- **Forward Chaining:** Starts from initial state and applies rules to reach the goal state.
- **Backward Chaining:** Starts from goal state and works backward to verify how it can be achieved.
- **Advantages:**
- **Efficient Exploration:** Reduces time by focusing on relevant states.
- **Optimized Solutions:** Heuristics guide the search towards optimal solutions.
- **Disadvantages:**
- **Resource Intensive:** Some strategies require high memory and computation.
- **Incomplete Search:** Heuristics might lead to local optima.

- **In Simple Hindi:**
  Search strategies ka use AI me solutions dhoondhne ke liye hota hai. Ye methods state space me search karte hain aur solution find karte hain.

- **BFS:** Har level par sabhi nodes ko explore karta hai.
- **DFS:** Ek branch ko pura explore karne ke baad backtrack karta hai.
- *A Search:* Ek smart strategy jo cost aur heuristic ka use karke solution dhoondhta hai.
- Control strategies decide karte hain ki hum kaunsa rasta pehle explore karenge:
- **Forward Chaining:** Initial state se goal state ki taraf kaam karte hain.
- **Backward Chaining:** Goal se shuru karte hain aur dekhte hain ki kaise waha pahunch sakte hain.

General Problem Solving

Definition (English):
- General problem solving refers to solving problems using a generalized approach that can be applied to a wide range of problems rather than a specific one.

Approach:
- **Formulation of Problem:** Define the problem clearly.
- **Solution Search:** Use algorithms to explore possible solutions.
- **Execution:** Apply the solution to achieve the goal.

Characteristics:
- **Versatile:** Can handle different types of problems.
- **Reusable Logic:** Same logic can be applied to solve various problems.

- **In Simple Hindi:**
  General problem solving ek aisi approach hai jisme hum kisi bhi problem ko solve karne ke liye ek general method ka use karte hain.
- **Problem ko define karna.**
- **Algorithm se solutions dhoondhna.**
- **Solution ko apply karna goal achieve karne ke liye.**

Production Systems

Definition (English):
A production system is a model of computation used for problem solving. It consists of a set of rules (productions), a database (working memory), and a control strategy to apply rules.

Components:

- **Rules (Productions):** If-Then conditions.
  Example:
  if (condition) then (action)
- **Working Memory:** Stores current state information.
- **Control Strategy:** Determines the order of rule application.
- **Types of Production Systems:**
- **Monotonic:** Rules do not contradict previously established facts.
- **Non-Monotonic:** Allows updating or changing facts based on new information.

Advantages:

- **Modular Design:** Easy to add or modify rules.
- **Adaptability:** Can handle dynamic environments.
- Disadvantages:
- **Complex Control:** Requires efficient strategies to avoid unnecessary rule applications.
- **Resource Usage:** High memory and computation demands.

- **In Simple Hindi:**
  Production system ek aisa model hai jo rules ka use karke problems solve karta hai. Ye system rules ke set aur working memory par kaam karta hai.
- **Rules:** Agar yeh condition true ho, to yeh action karo.
- **Working Memory:** Current state ka data store karta hai.
- **Control Strategy:** Decide karta hai kaunsa rule kab apply hoga.
- **Features:**
- **Easy to modify:** Naye rules asani se add ho sakte hain.
- **Dynamic Adaptation:** Nai information ke basis par facts update ho sakte hain.

Control Strategies: Forward and Backward Chaining

Forward Chaining (English):
- Forward chaining is a data-driven strategy used in inference engines. It starts from the initial state or given facts and applies inference rules to extract more data until the goal or solution is reached.

- **Steps of Forward Chaining:**

1. Start with known facts.
2. Apply applicable rules to infer new facts.
3. Repeat until the goal is achieved or no more rules can be applied.
- **Example:**
  If we know:
  Fact 1: All humans are mortal.
  Fact 2: Socrates is a human.
  Forward chaining will infer:
  Conclusion: Socrates is mortal.

Advantages:

- Works well with a large set of data.
- Automatically derives conclusions.

Disadvantages:
- May lead to unnecessary computations if irrelevant rules are applied.

- **Hindi Explanation:**

  Forward Chaining ek aisi technique hai jo known facts se shuruaat karti hai aur inference rules ka use karke naye facts derive karti hai jab tak goal state nahi mil jata.

  Example:

- Fact: Sabhi humans mortal hain.
- Socrates ek human hai.
  Forward chaining conclusion degi ki **Socrates mortal hai**.

Backward Chaining (English):
- Backward chaining is a goal-driven approach. It starts with the goal and works backward to find the initial facts that satisfy the goal.

- **Steps of Backward Chaining:**

1. Identify the goal.
2. Find rules that could lead to the goal.
3. Check if the conditions for these rules are met.
4. Repeat until all conditions are satisfied or no more rules apply.

- **Example:**
  Goal: Is Socrates mortal?
  Backward chaining will trace back to find that Socrates is human and all humans are mortal, confirming the goal.

  Advantages:
  - Focused search, avoiding unnecessary rules.
  - Effective when the goal is clearly defined.

  Disadvantages:
  - Can fail if the knowledge base lacks necessary facts.

- **Hindi Explanation:**
  Backward Chaining ek goal-driven approach hai jo pehle se define kiye gaye goal se shuruaat karke usko achieve karne ke liye required facts ko find karta hai.

- **Example:**
  Goal: Kya Socrates mortal hai?
  Backward chaining prove karega ki Socrates ek human hai aur sabhi humans mortal hote hain.

Exhaustive Searches: Depth-First and Breadth-First Search

Depth-First Search (DFS) (English):
- DFS explores as far as possible along each branch before backtracking. It uses a stack to remember the nodes to explore.

- **Steps:**
1. Start from the root node.
2. Explore each branch deeply before moving to the next branch.
3. Backtrack when a dead end is reached.

Advantages:
- Requires less memory.
- Finds a solution without exploring unnecessary nodes.

Disadvantages:
- May get stuck in infinite loops.
- Does not guarantee the shortest path.

- **Hindi Explanation:**
  DFS ek search technique hai jo ek branch ko pura explore karne ke baad hi backtrack karti hai.
- **Advantage:** Memory kam use hoti hai.
  Disadvantage: Infinite loops me atak sakti hai.

Breadth-First Search (BFS) (English):

- BFS explores all nodes at the current depth level before moving to nodes at the next level. It uses a queue to track nodes.

- **Steps:**

1. Start from the root node.
2. Explore all neighbors before moving deeper.
3. Repeat until the goal is found.

Advantages:

- Guarantees the shortest path.
- Explores level by level.

Disadvantages:

- High memory usage.
- Slower for deeper nodes.

Hindi Explanation:

BFS ek systematic approach hai jo har level ko explore karta hai.

Advantage: Sabse chhoti path guarantee karta hai.
Disadvantage: Zyada memory use karta hai.

Heuristic Search Techniques: Hill Climbing
Hill Climbing (English):

- Hill climbing is an optimization technique used in AI. It starts with an arbitrary solution and iteratively makes small changes to improve it.

- ## Types of Hill Climbing:

    1. **Simple Hill Climbing:** Moves to a better neighbor.
    2. **Steepest-Ascent Hill Climbing:** Evaluates all neighbors and moves to the best one.
    3. **Stochastic Hill Climbing:** Chooses a neighbor randomly.

    ## Advantages:
    - Simple and easy to implement.
    - Effective for local optimization.

    ## Disadvantages:
    - May get stuck in local maxima.
    - No guarantee of finding the global optimum.

- Hindi Explanation:

    Hill Climbing ek optimization method hai jo solution ko thoda-thoda better banata hai har step par.

- **Example:** Agar aap ek pahadi ke sabse upar pahunchna chahte hain, to har kadam par dekhte hain ki kaunsa next step aapko upar le ja sakta hai.

- **Exhaustive Searches: Depth-First Search (DFS) and Breadth-First Search (BFS)**

    Depth-First Search (DFS)
    - DFS is a search algorithm that explores as far down a branch as possible before backtracking. It uses a **stack** (can be implemented using recursion) to track the path.

    ## Features:

    - **Memory Efficiency:** Requires less memory as it stores only the current path.
    - **Backtracking:** Returns to previous nodes when a dead-end is encountered.
    - **Applications:** Useful for puzzles, maze-solving, etc.

    ### Advantages:
    - Low memory usage.
    - Finds a solution without exploring all nodes.

    ### Disadvantages:
    - May get stuck in infinite loops.
    - Doesn't guarantee the shortest path.

    - Hindi Explanations
    DFS ek aisi technique hai jo ek branch ko pura explore karti hai aur dead-end par backtrack karti hai.

Advantage: Memory efficient hoti hai.
Disadvantage: Chhoti path guarantee nahi karti.

- **Breadth-First Search (BFS)**
- BFS explores all nodes at the current depth before moving to the next level. It uses a **queue** for tracking.

- ## Features:

- **Guarantees Shortest Path:** If the path exists.
- **Explores Level by Level:** Ensures systematic exploration.

Advantages:
- Guarantees finding the shortest path.
- Completeness: Always finds a solution if one exists.

Disadvantages:
- Requires more memory.
- Slower for deep levels.

- **Hindi Explanation:**
  BFS systematically explore karta hai, sabhi neighbors ko pehle visit karta hai.

  Advantage: Chhoti path milti hai.
  Disadvantage: Zyada memory consume hoti hai.

- ## Heuristic Search Techniques

Hill Climbing
Hill climbing is an optimization algorithm that works iteratively, moving towards the goal by selecting the best neighboring state.

Types:
Simple Hill Climbing: Considers only immediate neighbors.
Steepest-Ascent Hill Climbing: Evaluates all neighbors and moves to the steepest ascent.
Stochastic Hill Climbing: Selects random neighbors to avoid local maxima.

Advantages:
- Simple to implement.
- Efficient for small problems.

Disadvantages:
- Stuck in **local maxima**.
- Doesn't guarantee global optimal solutions.

Hindi Explanation:
Hill Climbing ek iterative optimization technique hai jo har step par current solution ko improve karti hai.

Advantage: Simple implementation.
Disadvantage: Local maxima me atak sakti hai.

Branch and Bound Technique

Branch and Bound is a systematic search method that explores all branches of a tree but uses bounds to eliminate suboptimal solutions early.

Features:

- Systematically generates branches.
- Uses **upper and lower bounds** to prune the tree.

Advantages:
- Finds optimal solutions.
- Reduces unnecessary calculations.

Disadvantages:
- Computationally expensive.
- High memory usage.

Hindi Explanation:
Branch and Bound ek systematic algorithm hai jo tree ke branches ko explore karta hai aur un branches ko eliminate karta hai jo suboptimal solutions le jati hain.

Advantage: Optimal solution milti hai.
Disadvantage: Zyada computational resources lagti hain.

Best-First Search

Best-first search uses a priority queue to explore nodes based on a heuristic function. It selects the most promising node at each step.

Features:

- Uses **heuristic evaluation** to rank nodes.
- Combines advantages of both DFS and BFS.

Advantages:
- Reduces search time.
- Finds efficient solutions with good heuristics.

Disadvantages:
- Performance depends on the heuristic.
- Can be memory intensive.

Hindi Explanation:
Best-First Search ek heuristic-based algorithm hai jo har step par sabse promising node ko choose karta hai.

Advantage: Jaldi solutions milte hain agar heuristic sahi ho.
Disadvantage: Galat heuristic ke karan performance degrade ho sakti hai.

---

*A Algorithm**

- A* is a search algorithm that combines **path cost** and **heuristics** to find the most optimal path.
  Formula Used: $f(n) = g(n) + h(n)$
  Where:
  $g(n)$: Cost to reach the current node.
  $h(n)$: Estimated cost to reach the goal from the current node.
  $f(n)$: Total cost.

Features:
- Combines benefits of DFS, BFS.
- Guarantees optimal solutions if the heuristic is admissible.

Advantages:
- Guarantees the shortest path.
- Flexible with multiple goals.

Disadvantages:
- High memory usage.
- Performance depends on heuristic quality.

Hindi Explanation:
A* ek heuristic-based algorithm hai jo cost aur heuristic ka combination use karta hai goal tak ki sabse efficient path find karne ke liye.

Formula:
$f(n) = g(n) + h(n)$
Advantage: Optimal solution guarantee karta hai.
Disadvantage: High memory aur computation lagti hai.

AND/OR Graphs

AND/OR graphs are a special type of directed graph used to represent problems that involve decision-making with multiple interdependent subproblems.

Key Features:
1. **AND Nodes**: These represent problems where all child nodes must be solved to solve the parent node.
2. **OR Nodes**: These represent problems where solving any one child node solves the parent node.

Applications:
- **Game theory**: For solving games with complex strategies.
- **Planning systems**: For tasks that can be broken down into sub-tasks.

Advantages:
- Helps model complex problems with dependencies.
- Provides a structured approach to problem-solving.

Disadvantages:
- Can be computationally expensive for large graphs.

- **Hindi Explanation**:

  AND/OR Graphs un problems ko model karte hain jahan multiple decisions aur sub-problems involved hote hain.

- **AND nodes**: Sabhi sub-problems ko solve karna zaruri hota hai.

- **OR nodes**: Kisi ek sub-problem ko solve karna kaafi hota hai.

  Advantage: Complex problems ko simplify karta hai.
  Disadvantage: Badi problems me zyada computation lagta hai.

Problem Reduction and AO Algorithm*

The **AO*** (AND/OR) algorithm is an extension of the A* algorithm, designed to solve problems represented by AND/OR graphs. It uses heuristics to find an optimal solution by reducing the problem.

Steps in AO*:
1. **Start at the root node**.
2. Expand nodes based on heuristics.
3. Solve subproblems (AND nodes) or select optimal solutions (OR nodes).
4. Update costs and backtrack to adjust the solution path.

Applications:
- Solves decision-making problems in AI.
- Useful in **game trees** and **planning**.

Advantages:
- Finds optimal solutions efficiently.
- Reduces unnecessary calculations by pruning suboptimal branches.

Disadvantages:
- Performance heavily depends on the quality of the heuristic.
- Computationally intensive for large graphs.

- **Hindi Explanation**:
  AO* ek heuristic-based algorithm hai jo AND/OR graph me problems ko solve karta hai.

  Process:
  1. Root se start karke best path choose karta hai.
  2. Subproblems solve karke optimal solution find karta hai.

  Advantage: Efficiently optimal solution milta hai.
  Disadvantage: Galat heuristic par performance degrade ho sakti hai.

Constraint Satisfaction Problems (CSPs)

CSPs involve finding a solution that satisfies a set of constraints or conditions. These problems are common in areas like **scheduling**, **resource allocation**, and **puzzle solving**.

Components:

1. **Variables**: The elements to be assigned values.
2. **Domains**: Possible values for each variable.
3. **Constraints**: Rules that must be satisfied.

Examples:
- **Sudoku**: Each number must appear only once in a row, column, and box.
- **Timetable Scheduling**: No two classes can be scheduled in the same room at the same time.

Advantages:
- Provides a clear framework for solving structured problems.
- Many efficient algorithms, such as **backtracking** and **constraint propagation**, are available.

Disadvantages:
- Can be computationally intensive for large or highly constrained problems.
- May require sophisticated heuristics for efficient solving.

- **Hindi Explanation**:
  Constraint Satisfaction Problems (CSPs) wo problems hain jisme variables ke liye aisi values find karni hoti hain jo sabhi constraints ko satisfy karein.

  Example:
- **Sudoku**: Ek specific rule ke hisaab se numbers ko arrange karna.

  Advantage: Efficient framework provide karta hai.
  Disadvantage: Large problems me zyada computation lagta hai.

Knowledge Representation

- **Knowledge Representation (KR)** refers to how knowledge about the world can be represented in a way that a computer system can utilize to solve complex tasks. The goal is to allow systems to draw inferences or make decisions.

First-Order Predicate Calculus (FOPC)

- FOPC is a formal language used to represent facts and relationships about objects. It extends **propositional logic** by including:

- **Variables**: Represent objects (e.g., x, y).
- **Predicates**: Represent relationships (e.g., Likes(Alice, Pizza)).

    Quantifiers:
    - **Universal Quantifier ($\forall$)**: Applies to all objects.
    - **Existential Quantifier ($\exists$)**: Applies to at least one object.

Features:
- Expresses facts involving objects and their relationships.
- Provides a powerful tool for reasoning.

Advantages:

- Highly expressive.
- Supports complex reasoning.

Disadvantages:

- Can be computationally expensive.

- Requires proper handling of variables.

- **Hindi Explanation**:

  FOPC ek logical system hai jo objects aur unke relations ko represent karta hai. Isme variables aur predicates ka use hota hai.

- **Advantage**: Complex relationships ko express karna aasaan hota hai.
- **Disadvantage**: Computation intensive ho sakta hai.

Skolemization

- **Skolemization** is a process used in logic to eliminate **existential quantifiers** by introducing a **Skolem function** or **constant**.

Purpose:
- Simplifies logical expressions for easier processing by automated systems.

- **Example**: For a statement like:
  $\exists x\, P(x)$
  It introduces a constant **c** such that:
  $P(c)$

Advantages:
- Simplifies expressions.
- Facilitates resolution-based theorem proving.

Disadvantages:
- May increase the complexity of some proofs.

Hindi Explanation:

Skolemization ka upyog existential quantifiers ko eliminate karne ke liye hota hai, taki logical expressions ko simplify kiya ja sake.

- **Advantage**: Proof process ko asaan banata hai.
- **Disadvantage**: Kabhi-kabhi proof complex ho sakta hai.

Resolution Principle & Unification

- **Resolution Principle** is a rule of inference used for automated theorem proving.
  Unification is a process of making two logical expressions identical by substituting variables.

Steps in Resolution:
1. Convert statements to **clausal form**.
2. Use the resolution rule to derive contradictions.

Advantages:
- Basis for many AI inference engines.
- Systematic and powerful for logical proofs.

Disadvantages:
- Can become computationally expensive.

- **Hindi Explanation**:

  Resolution principle ka use logical proofs ke liye hota hai jaha contradictions ko derive kiya jata hai. **Unification** ka kaam logical terms ko match karna hai.

- **Advantage**: Systematic logical reasoning.
- **Disadvantage**: Zyada computation ki zarurat hoti hai.

Interface Mechanisms: Horn's Clauses

Horn's Clauses are a special form of clauses used in logic programming and Prolog.
A Horn clause has at most one positive literal.

Advantages:
- Efficient for computation.
- Useful in logic programming.

Disadvantages:
- Limited expressiveness.

Semantic Networks

- A **semantic network** is a graph structure representing knowledge in nodes (concepts) and edges (relationships).

Features:
- Represents hierarchical relationships.
- Supports inheritance of properties.

Applications:
- **Natural Language Processing** (NLP).
- **Expert systems**.

- **Hindi Explanation**:
  Semantic Network ek graph structure hai jo nodes aur edges ke madhyam se knowledge represent karta hai.

- **Advantage**: Concepts aur relations ko easily dikhata hai.
- **Disadvantage**: Complex queries ke liye kam effective.

Frame Systems and Value Inheritance

- **Frame Systems** are structures used in artificial intelligence for representing stereotypical knowledge about objects or situations. They are used to capture knowledge in a way that is easy to understand and manipulate.

Frame Systems:

- A **frame** is essentially a data structure that holds information about a particular concept or object. It consists of a collection of attributes (or slots), each with a value that describes the object or concept in question.

- Example:
    - **Frame for "Car"**:
        - Slots: Color, Type, Engine Capacity, Manufacturer
        - Values: Red, Sedan, 2.0L, Toyota

- Frames are used for knowledge representation, where an object is defined by its properties (slots), and each slot can have a value associated with it.

Value Inheritance:

- **Value inheritance** refers to the mechanism by which a subclass or more specific frame can inherit attributes from a more general or parent frame.

- Example:
    - **Frame for "Vehicle"** might have slots like: "Wheels", "Fuel Type", and "Capacity".
    - **Frame for "Car"** inherits these attributes but adds its own specific details (like "Car Type", "Engine Type").
- This inheritance allows for the reuse of knowledge, making the system more efficient and organized.

Advantages:

- **Efficiency**: Reduces redundancy by allowing values to be inherited from parent frames.
- **Organization**: Helps in organizing knowledge hierarchically, making it easier to manage and extend.

Disadvantages:

- **Complexity**: Inheritance hierarchies can become complex if not well-organized.
- **Limited Flexibility**: If not properly structured, frames might lack flexibility in representing all possible relationships.

Hindi Explanation:

Frame Systems ek data structure hai jisme objects ya situations ke baare mein stereotype knowledge store ki jaati hai. Ye ek object ke attributes ko represent karta hai, jaise ki color, size, type, etc.
- **Value Inheritance** ka matlab hai ki ek frame apne parent frame se values inherit kar leta hai. Jaise ek "Car" frame apne parent "Vehicle" frame se wheels, fuel type, aur capacity ko inherit kar leta hai.
- **Advantage**: Ye system ko organize karta hai aur redundancy ko reduce karta hai.
- **Disadvantage**: Agar inheritance structure properly nahi banaya gaya ho, toh yeh system complex ho sakta hai.

Scripts & Conceptual Dependency

Scripts:
- A **script** is a knowledge representation structure that represents stereotypical sequences of events or actions that typically occur in a given situation. It's used to model common scenarios in everyday life, such as going to a restaurant, traveling to a hotel, or shopping.

Key Features:

- Scripts are used to represent **sequences of events** that are expected to happen in a particular context.
- They include **default values** and rules for filling in any missing information.

Example:
Restaurant Script:
1. Enter restaurant.
2. Wait to be seated.
3. Order food.
4. Eat food.
5. Pay the bill.
6. Leave restaurant.

- Scripts help systems like **natural language processing** or **robotics** to understand and simulate real-world behavior.

Conceptual Dependency:

- **Conceptual Dependency (CD)** is a theory used in AI for representing the meaning of natural language sentences at a deeper conceptual level. Unlike traditional sentence structure, **CD** focuses on the action and the relationships between objects and actors involved.

- It abstracts away from the actual words used in a sentence and captures the **underlying meaning**.

- **Example**:
- **Sentence**: "John gave Mary a book."

- **CD Representation**:
    - **Action**: Give
    - **Agent**: John
    - **Recipient**: Mary
    - **Object**: Book

Advantages of Scripts and Conceptual Dependency:

- **Understanding Context**: Scripts help AI systems understand real-world scenarios and their typical sequences.
- **Language Processing**: CD helps in breaking down complex sentences into simpler, more understandable concepts, making it easier to interpret natural language.

Disadvantages:

- **Limited Coverage**: Scripts are limited to typical situations and cannot handle novel or unexpected events well.
- **Complexity in Representation**: For more complex events or actions, scripts can become large and difficult to manage.

- **Hindi Explanation**:

    Scripts ek knowledge representation structure hai jo kisi situation mein hone wale events ya actions ke sequences ko dikhata hai. Jaise restaurant jaane ki script mein pehle restaurant mein enter karna, phir seat milna, order dena, khana khana, bill pay karna aur restaurant se nikalna hota hai.

- **Conceptual Dependency** ek theory hai jisme natural language sentences ke meanings ko ek conceptual level pe represent kiya jata hai. Isme hum actions aur unme involved objects ke relations ko samajhte hain, na ki words ka structure.

- **Advantage**: Ye help karta hai systems ko context samajhne mein aur language ko interpret karne mein.

- **Disadvantage**: Agar scenario novel ho ya unexpected ho, toh scripts utni effective nahi hoti hain.

Natural Language Processing (NLP) Parsing Techniques

- **Parsing** is the process of analyzing a string of symbols, either in natural language or in programming language, according to the rules of formal grammar. It involves determining the grammatical structure of a sentence, which is crucial for understanding the meaning of the sentence.

Parsing Techniques:

1. **Top-Down Parsing**:
    - Starts from the root of the parse tree and works down to the leaves.
    - It tries to find a match for the input sentence by expanding the grammar rules from the start symbol.
    - Example: If the input is a sentence, the top-down parser begins with the sentence and breaks it down into its components.
2. **Bottom-Up Parsing**:
    - Starts from the leaves (words) and builds up to the root.
    - It looks for subcomponents and gradually combines them to form larger constituents.
    - Example: If we are given individual words, the bottom-up parser begins with words and attempts to combine them into phrases and then sentences.
3. **Earley Parsing**:
    - A more sophisticated parsing technique that works in a **dynamic programming** manner.
    - It works well for all context-free grammars and is especially effective for parsing ambiguous grammars.

4. **Chart Parsing**:
    - This technique uses a chart to store the intermediate results of the parsing process to avoid redundant parsing of the same substrings.

Hindi Explanation:

- **Parsing** ek process hai jisme hum kisi string ko grammar ke rules ke hisaab se analyze karte hain. Ye process sentence ke grammatical structure ko samajhne mein madad karta hai.
- **Top-Down Parsing**: Isme hum sentence ke root se start karte hain aur subcomponents ko identify karte hain.
- **Bottom-Up Parsing**: Isme hum words se start karte hain aur phir unhe combine karte hue sentence banate hain.

Context-Free Grammar (CFG)

- A **Context-Free Grammar (CFG)** is a formal grammar used to describe the syntax of programming languages and natural languages. In CFG, the left-hand side of every production rule is a single non-terminal symbol, and the right-hand side is a sequence of terminals and/or non-terminals.

Components of CFG:

- **Terminals**: The actual symbols of the language (words or characters).
- **Non-Terminals**: Symbols used to define the structure of the language.

- **Production Rules**: The rules that describe how non-terminals can be replaced by combinations of terminals and non-terminals.
- **Start Symbol**: The non-terminal from where the production process begins.

- **Example**:
  S → NP VP
  NP → Det Noun
  VP → Verb NP
  Det → the | a
  Noun → dog | cat
  Verb → chases | sees
- **Example Sentence**: "The dog chases the cat."
- Here, the sentence can be parsed using the production rules defined by the CFG.

Hindi Explanation:

- **Context-Free Grammar (CFG)** ek formal grammar hai jo language ke syntax ko define karta hai. Isme har production rule mein left side ek non-terminal symbol hota hai, aur right side mein terminals ya non-terminals ho sakte hain.

  Example:
- **S** (Sentence) ko **NP** (Noun Phrase) aur **VP** (Verb Phrase) se replace kiya ja sakta hai.

Recursive Transition Nets (RTN)

- **Recursive Transition Nets (RTNs)** are a formalism used in syntactic analysis of natural language. They extend finite state machines and are used to describe recursive structures in languages.
- RTNs are represented as a set of states and transitions that recursively reference themselves.
- **Recursive** means that an RTN can reference its own structure, making it capable of describing complex nested structures like phrases within sentences.
- RTNs are especially useful for parsing **recursive** structures in **natural languages** like noun phrases or embedded clauses.
- **Example**:
- A sentence like "The cat that chased the mouse ran away."
- RTNs can handle recursive structures by defining rules for noun phrases and sub-clauses recursively.

Hindi Explanation:
- **Recursive Transition Nets (RTNs)** ek formal system hai jo natural language ki syntax ko analyze karne ke liye use hota hai. Isme recursive structures ko define kiya ja sakta hai, jaise noun phrases ya clauses ko nested form mein.

Augmented Transition Nets (ATN)

- **Augmented Transition Nets (ATNs)** are an extension of RTNs and are used in natural language processing to model **syntactic structures**. They augment RTNs by adding **action rules** which allow for the **processing of additional information** during parsing, like **semantic actions** or additional context.
- ATNs have a **state transition model** that is enhanced with actions that can occur as a result of transitions between states.
- These actions can involve **semantic processing**, like assigning meanings to words or phrases as they are encountered.
- **Example**:
- In a sentence like "John eats the apple," an ATN would not only parse the sentence structure but also associate "John" with the subject and "eats" with the action verb.

Hindi Explanation:
- **Augmented Transition Nets (ATNs)** ek extension hai RTNs ka, jo natural language processing mein use hota hai. Isme **action rules** add kiye jaate hain, jo parsing ke dauran additional information process karte hain, jaise semantic actions.

Case and Logic Grammars
- **Case Grammar** and **Logic Grammar** are used to describe how the different parts of a sentence (like subject, object, verb, etc.) are related to each other based on their **roles** or **cases**.

Case Grammar:
- Case grammar focuses on the **roles** played by different parts of a sentence, like **subject**, **object**, and **verb**.

- It associates a case with each noun in a sentence, such as **nominative** (subject), **accusative** (object), or **genitive** (possessor).

- **Example**:
- "John (subject) gave the book (object) to Mary (recipient)."
    - **John** is in the nominative case (subject),
    - **The book** is in the accusative case (object),
    - **Mary** is in the dative case (recipient).

Logic Grammar:
- **Logic grammar** applies logical symbols and expressions to represent relationships between words in sentences. It is based on **predicate logic** and defines syntactic structures in terms of logical operations.

Semantic Analysis

- **Semantic Analysis** is the process of **interpreting** the meanings of words, phrases, or sentences in context, beyond just syntactic structure. It focuses on understanding **intentions**, **ambiguities**, and relationships between elements.

Key Goals:
- **Disambiguation**: Resolving ambiguities in word meanings based on context.
- **Understanding Relationships**: Analyzing how words relate to one another and their roles in the sentence.
- **Semantic Representation**: Creating a representation of the meaning of a sentence in a machine-understandable form.

Hindi Explanation:
- **Semantic Analysis** ka mtlb hai ki hum sentence ke meaning ko samajhte hain, na ki sirf uske grammatical structure ko. Isme hum words ke meaning ko context ke hisaab se resolve karte hain aur sentence mein elements ke beech relationship ko samajhte hain.

Game Playing

- **Game playing** is one of the most studied topics in **artificial intelligence (AI)**. It involves designing systems that can play games such as chess, checkers, or tic-tac-toe, and it provides insights into decision-making and strategy. The goal is for the AI to make optimal decisions in a competitive environment.

Minimax Search Procedure:

- The **Minimax** algorithm is a decision-making strategy used in two-player, zero-sum games (where one player's gain is another player's loss). The algorithm aims to minimize the possible loss for a worst-case scenario. It is typically used to determine the best possible move for the player assuming the opponent also plays optimally.

Steps of Minimax Algorithm:

1. **Generate all possible moves** for both players.
2. **Evaluate the terminal states** (game over scenarios like win, lose, draw).
3. **Minimax value**: The value of the current node is determined based on the worst-case scenario:
    - For the **maximizing player** (the player making the current move), it selects the move with the highest value.
    - For the **minimizing player** (the opponent), it selects the move with the lowest value.
4. The algorithm recursively evaluates all possible game states until it reaches the terminal states and then selects the optimal move.

- **Example**: In **tic-tac-toe**, the algorithm will look at all possible game states, evaluate them, and choose the best move based on the Minimax strategy.

Alpha-Beta Cutoffs:

- **Alpha-Beta Pruning** is an optimization technique for the Minimax algorithm. It reduces the number of nodes that need to be evaluated in the search tree, which makes the search process more efficient.

- **Working of Alpha-Beta Pruning**:

- It maintains two values: **alpha** and **beta**.
    - **Alpha** is the best value that the maximizer can guarantee at that point.
    - **Beta** is the best value that the minimizer can guarantee.

- As the algorithm searches through the tree, it "prunes" branches where further exploration is unnecessary:

    - If the value of a node is greater than **beta**, the minimizer will avoid considering that node (because the opponent will never let the game reach that state).
    - If the value of a node is less than **alpha**, the maximizer will avoid considering that node.

- By cutting off branches early, **alpha-beta pruning** makes the search much faster, improving the performance of Minimax by a significant factor.

Additional Refinements:

1. **Iterative Deepening**:
    - A hybrid search strategy that combines the benefits of depth-first search and breadth-first search.
    - The algorithm searches at increasing depths, starting from depth 1 and going deeper each time.
    - This helps ensure that the search tree is explored up to a certain depth limit and improves the chances of finding an optimal solution within that limit.
2. **Transposition Tables**:
    - These are used to store previously computed values of game states to avoid redundant calculations.
    - This helps to optimize the algorithm by recognizing already-visited states and using previously computed results.

Planning

- **Planning** in AI refers to the process of deciding on a sequence of actions that will lead to the desired goal. It involves creating a plan to achieve an objective by considering various possible actions and their consequences.

Overview of Planning:

- Planning is a critical aspect of AI, where the system must figure out how to reach a goal by performing specific actions. A **planning problem** involves a starting state, a goal state, and a set of possible actions that can change the state.

- **Types of Planning**:

1. **Goal-Oriented Planning**: The AI system plans based on a set goal and searches for the actions that will lead to that goal.
2. **Problem-Solving**: Planning can also be seen as solving a problem where the goal is to determine a sequence of actions that leads from the initial state to the goal state.

Example Domain: The Block World:

- The **Block World** is a classic example in AI planning. In this domain, blocks are stacked in various configurations, and the goal is to move the blocks from one configuration to another.

The actions in this domain include picking up a block and placing it on top of another block or the table.

- For example, consider the following initial configuration of blocks:
  A is on the table.
  B is on top of A.
  C is on top of B.

- The goal could be to move all blocks so that **C** is on top of **A**, and **B** is on the table.
- The planning problem involves finding a sequence of actions to achieve this goal, like moving **C** off **B**, then moving **B** onto the table, and so on.

Components of Planning Systems:

- A **planning system** consists of several components:
1. **Initial State**: The starting configuration or condition of the world.
2. **Goal State**: The desired configuration or condition of the world.
3. **Actions**: The operations that can be performed to change the state.
4. **State Transition Model**: Defines how each action changes the world from one state to another.
5. **Plan**: A sequence of actions that transforms the initial state into the goal state.

Goal Stack Planning:

- **Goal Stack Planning** is a technique used for AI planning where the system uses a stack data structure to maintain and process the goals. In this technique, the planner works on goals by pushing them onto a stack. It starts by focusing on the top-most goal and breaks it down into subgoals, which are then added to the stack. The planner continues this process until all the subgoals are resolved.

- **Advantages**:
    - Easy to implement and understand.
    - Useful for problems that can be divided into sub-goals.
- **Disadvantages**:
    - Does not scale well for complex problems with a large number of goals.

Non-linear Planning:

- **Non-linear Planning** refers to a planning approach where actions are not executed in a fixed sequence. Unlike traditional planning, where actions are taken one after another, non-linear planning allows for actions to overlap, meaning that some actions may be executed out of order as long as they don't conflict.

- For example, in a real-world scenario like a car trip, you could plan to:
- Pack bags.
- Start the car.
- Get the keys.

- In a linear plan, these actions must happen in sequence. But in a non-linear plan, actions such as packing bags and starting the car could happen simultaneously, depending on the context.

- **Advantages**:
- Allows for greater flexibility in planning.
- Reduces the overall time taken to reach the goal.

Hindi Explanation:

Game Playing:
- **Game Playing** mein AI system ko games khelne ke liye banaya jata hai. Iska main purpose hota hai optimal decision lena, jaise ki chess ya tic-tac-toe mein hota hai.
- **Minimax Search Procedure** ek algorithm hai jo do-player ke zero-sum games mein use hota hai. Isme, ek player apne liye best move choose karta hai, aur opponent ke liye worst case ko minimize karta hai.
- **Alpha-Beta Cutoffs** Minimax ke optimization hain jo unnecessary nodes ko evaluate karne se rok dete hain, isse search speed improve hoti hai.

Planning:
- **Planning** AI ka ek process hai jisme system ko apne goals ko achieve karne ke liye actions ka sequence decide karna hota hai.
- **Goal Stack Planning** ek technique hai jisme goals ko stack mein rakha jata hai aur unhe step by step solve kiya jata hai.
- **Non-linear Planning** mein, actions ko ek sequence mein nahi, balki parallel execute kiya jata hai jab tak ki unme koi conflict na ho.

UNIT-5

Probabilistic Reasoning and Uncertainty

- **Probabilistic Reasoning** is a technique used to deal with uncertainty in AI systems. In real-world situations, decisions are often made under uncertainty, meaning that the available information is incomplete or ambiguous. Probabilistic reasoning uses probability theory to manage this uncertainty and make informed decisions.

Probability Theory:

- Probability theory is a branch of mathematics that deals with the likelihood of different outcomes occurring. In AI, probability theory helps in quantifying uncertainty and enables systems to make predictions about events or situations.

Basic Concepts:

- **Probability**: A number between 0 and 1 that represents the likelihood of an event occurring.
    - If the probability is 1, the event is certain to happen.
    - If the probability is 0, the event will not happen.
- **Conditional Probability**: The probability of an event occurring, given that another event has already occurred.
- For example, if there is a 70% chance it will rain today, the probability is 0.7. If the probability of rain is conditional on the

temperature being above 30°C, this is an example of conditional probability.

Bayes' Theorem and Bayesian Networks:

- **Bayes' Theorem** is a mathematical formula that allows us to update the probability estimate for a hypothesis based on new evidence. It is a powerful tool for probabilistic reasoning, particularly in uncertain situations.

- **Bayes' Theorem**:

$$P(H|E) = \frac{P(E|H) \cdot P(H)}{P(E)}$$

Where:

- $P(H|E)$ is the probability of the hypothesis H given the evidence E.

- $P(E|H)$ is the probability of the evidence E given the hypothesis H.

- $P(H)$ is the prior probability of the hypothesis.

- $P(E)$ is the probability of the evidence.

Example: If we want to predict the likelihood of a person being ill (hypothesis H) based on a positive result from a medical test (evidence E), Bayes' theorem helps in adjusting our belief based on prior knowledge (such as the likelihood of the disease in the general population and the accuracy of the test).

Bayesian Networks: Bayesian Networks are graphical models that represent a set of variables and their probabilistic dependencies. In these networks, nodes represent variables, and edges represent the probabilistic relationships between them.

They are particularly useful for making decisions under uncertainty and are widely used in machine learning and expert systems.

Example: In a Bayesian network for medical diagnosis, nodes might represent symptoms (fever, cough, etc.), diseases (cold, flu), and test results. The network allows the system to calculate the probability of a certain disease based on observed symptoms and test results.

Certainty Factor:

- A **Certainty Factor (CF)** is a value that indicates the confidence level of a belief or hypothesis in expert systems. It is often used in **expert systems** to represent the certainty with which the system makes a particular inference or decision.

- **Features**:

- The **certainty factor** is typically a number between 0 and 1 (sometimes, it can be a value between -1 and 1).

    - A CF of 0 means no certainty (or complete uncertainty).
    - A CF of 1 means full certainty.
    - Negative values indicate negative certainty (i.e., the hypothesis is unlikely).

- In expert systems, the certainty factor helps in combining multiple pieces of evidence to form a final decision. For example, if two pieces of evidence are both weakly supportive of a diagnosis, the system may adjust the certainty factor accordingly.

Expert Systems

- **Expert Systems** are AI systems designed to mimic the decision-making ability of a human expert in a specific domain. They use a knowledge base of facts and rules, along with inference mechanisms, to solve complex problems that usually require human expertise.

Introduction to Expert Systems:

- An **Expert System** is a computer system that emulates the decision-making ability of a human expert in solving complex problems. It consists of:

1. **Knowledge Base**: A collection of facts and rules that represent knowledge in a specific domain.

2. **Inference Engine**: The mechanism that processes the knowledge base to infer new facts or make decisions.

3. **User Interface**: Allows users to interact with the system.

4. **Explanation System**: Explains the reasoning behind the system's conclusions to the user.

- Expert systems are typically used in domains such as medicine, engineering, finance, and customer support. They offer a reliable way of providing expert-level decisions, especially when human expertise is not available.

- **Example**: In the medical field, an expert system can assist doctors in diagnosing diseases based on symptoms and medical history. It can use a rule-based system, where rules like "If the patient has a fever and cough, the likelihood of flu is high" are applied to reach conclusions.

Applications of Expert Systems:

1. **Medical Diagnosis**: Expert systems are used to help doctors diagnose diseases by analyzing symptoms, medical history, and test results.

2. **Customer Support**: Expert systems can help answer customer queries by simulating the expertise of a support agent.

3. **Engineering Design**: Expert systems can assist in designing systems or products by applying engineering principles and rules.

4. **Finance and Investment**: Expert systems are used for risk analysis, stock market predictions, and financial planning.

5. **Troubleshooting**: Expert systems can be used for diagnosing problems in machines or systems, offering solutions based on expert knowledge.

Advantages and Disadvantages of Expert Systems:

Advantages:

1. **Availability of Expertise**: Expert systems can provide expert-level advice anytime, unlike human experts who are available only during specific hours.

2. **Consistency**: Expert systems provide consistent answers since they always follow the same set of rules and logic.

3. **Efficiency**: Expert systems can solve problems faster than human experts, especially in complex scenarios with large amounts of data.

4. **Cost-Effective**: They can reduce the need for highly skilled professionals in some areas, thus reducing costs.

Disadvantages:

1. **Limited Knowledge**: Expert systems are only as good as the knowledge base they are built upon. If the knowledge base is incomplete or outdated, the system's performance will be limited.

2. **Lack of Flexibility**: Expert systems are rigid and cannot handle scenarios outside their programmed knowledge or rules.

3. **No Creativity**: Unlike human experts, expert systems cannot come up with innovative solutions or ideas.

4. **High Development Cost**: Developing an expert system requires significant investment in knowledge acquisition, system design, and testing.

Hindi Explanation:

Probabilistic Reasoning and Uncertainty:

- **Probabilistic Reasoning** ka use hum un situations mein karte hain jahan humein uncertainty ya confusion hota hai. Jab humare paas poori information nahi hoti, to **Probability Theory** ka use karke hum kisi bhi event ke hone ki sambhavana (likelihood) ko jaanchte hain.

- **Bayes' Theorem** ek formula hai jo humein naye evidence ke aadhar par apne purane assumptions ko update karne mein madad karta hai. Isse hum apne decision-making ko improve kar sakte hain jab naye data ya information milti hai.

- **Certainty Factor** ek number hota hai jo kisi bhi decision ke prati system ke bharose ko darshata hai. Jab certainty factor zyada hota hai, to system ko apne decision par vishwas hota hai.

Expert Systems:

- **Expert Systems** ek AI application hai jo kisi specific domain mein human experts ke decision-making ko imitate karta hai. Yeh systems knowledge base aur inference engine ka use karke complex problems solve karte hain.

- **Applications** mein expert systems ka use medical diagnosis, customer support, engineering design, aur financial planning jaise kai domains mein hota hai. Yeh systems human experts ko assist karte hain, unka kaam asaan banate hain aur unke decision-making process ko automate karte hain.

- **Advantages** mein inki availability, consistency, aur efficiency shamil hai, jabki **Disadvantages** mein unka limited knowledge aur lack of flexibility hai.

Expert System Shells

1. An **Expert System Shell** is a pre-packaged software framework that provides the necessary tools and infrastructure for building expert systems. These shells allow users to design, develop, and implement expert systems without needing to build everything from scratch. Expert system shells provide the core components like the inference engine, user interface, and knowledge base framework, which can be customized as per the needs of the specific application.

Features of Expert System Shells:

- **Inference Engine**: It applies logical reasoning to the knowledge base to draw conclusions or make decisions.

- **Knowledge Base**: It stores domain-specific knowledge, typically in the form of rules or facts.

- **User Interface**: It allows the user to interact with the system, providing inputs and receiving outputs.

- **Explanation Facilities**: It can explain how a conclusion was reached based on the rules and facts in the knowledge base.

Advantages:

2. **Faster Development**: By using pre-built components, expert system shells allow faster system development.

3. **Easy Customization**: Users can modify the shell to cater to the needs of specific domains.

4. **Cost-effective**: Reduces the cost of building an expert system from scratch.

5.

Disadvantages:

1. **Limited Flexibility**: Some shells may not provide the flexibility required for highly specialized tasks.

2. **Requires Expertise**: Although shells provide a framework, they still require domain knowledge to design effective systems.

3. **Dependency on Shell Vendor**: The system may be restricted to the features provided by the shell.

Vidwan Framework

6. **Vidwan** is a framework for expert systems that specifically focuses on acquiring, representing, and reasoning about knowledge. It provides a structured approach to building knowledge-based systems, with an emphasis on knowledge representation, inference mechanisms, and the integration of the system into a larger environment.

Key Features:

- **Knowledge Representation**: Vidwan provides an advanced structure for representing complex knowledge in a format that an AI system can process.

- **Inference Mechanism**: Uses logical rules or probabilistic reasoning to derive conclusions from the knowledge base.

- **Integration**: Designed to integrate with other systems and databases for seamless data exchange and decision-making.

Importance:

- Vidwan helps automate the process of capturing expert knowledge and using that knowledge to solve problems, making it valuable in complex domains such as medical diagnosis or technical troubleshooting.

Applications:

- Widely used in fields such as **medicine**, **finance**, and **engineering**, where expert knowledge is crucial for decision-making.

Knowledge Acquisition

Knowledge Acquisition refers to the process of gathering knowledge from various sources to populate the knowledge base of an expert system. This is a critical phase in developing an expert system because the quality and accuracy of the knowledge base directly affect the system's performance.

Methods of Knowledge Acquisition:

1. **Interviews with Experts**: Knowledge is gathered by interacting with human experts who provide their insights into the problem domain.

2. **Documentation Review**: Analyzing existing documents, manuals, books, and research papers to extract relevant knowledge.

3. **Observations**: Observing how experts solve problems in real-world scenarios and recording their approaches.

Challenges:

- **Complexity**: The process of capturing complex knowledge from experts can be time-consuming and challenging.

- **Consistency**: Ensuring that the knowledge is consistent and error-free across the entire knowledge base.

Case Studies:

Case studies are detailed analyses of specific instances or problems that help in understanding how expert systems work in real-life situations. Case studies provide valuable insight into the practical application of expert systems, helping to highlight their effectiveness and limitations.

MYCIN: A case study of an expert system, **MYCIN**, was developed in the 1970s to diagnose bacterial infections and recommend treatments. MYCIN was one of the earliest successful applications of expert systems in the medical field.

MYCIN Features:

- **Knowledge Base**: MYCIN used a set of rules to determine the appropriate diagnosis based on patient symptoms and test results.

- **Inference Mechanism**: The system used forward chaining to apply the rules and generate conclusions.

- **User Interaction**: Doctors or healthcare professionals would input patient data, and MYCIN would provide recommendations for treatment.

MYCIN is considered an early success in the field of expert systems and served as a model for subsequent systems.

Learning Methods in AI

AI systems, including expert systems, often use various **learning techniques** to improve their performance over time or to adapt to new situations. These learning methods include **rote learning**, **inductive learning**, and **explanation-based learning**.

Rote Learning:

> **Rote learning** is a method where the system memorizes specific examples or facts and uses them to make decisions. In this approach, the system does not understand the underlying patterns or rules but simply recalls previous experiences.

- **Example**: In an expert system for medical diagnosis, rote learning might involve remembering specific diagnoses and treatments for a particular set of symptoms.

Inductive Learning:

> In **inductive learning**, the system learns patterns or rules from a set of examples. It generalizes from the examples to create a rule that can be applied to new, unseen cases. This approach allows the system to infer knowledge from specific observations.

- **Example**: A system could learn that "if a patient has a fever and cough, it is likely they have the flu" based on past data.

Explanation-Based Learning:

Explanation-based learning involves the system improving its knowledge by analyzing explanations for why certain decisions were made. The system refines its decision-making process based on these explanations and applies them to future cases.

- **Example**: In a diagnostic expert system, the system could analyze why a certain treatment worked and learn to apply that knowledge to similar future cases.

Hindi Explanation:

Expert System Shells:

Expert System Shells ek pre-packaged software framework hai jo expert system banane ke liye necessary tools aur infrastructure provide karta hai. Iska use karke hum apne domain ke liye custom expert system develop kar sakte hain bina sab kuch zero se start kiye. Expert system shells mein core components hote hain jaise inference engine, user interface, aur knowledge base framework.

Vidwan Framework:

Vidwan Framework ek aisa framework hai jo knowledge acquire karne aur represent karne mein madad karta hai. Iska use complex knowledge ko system mein integrate karne ke liye kiya jata hai. Yeh mostly medical aur technical domains mein use hota hai.

Knowledge Acquisition:

Knowledge Acquisition ka matlab hai experts se knowledge acquire karna, jo knowledge base ko fill karta hai. Yeh process interviews, documentation review, aur direct observation se kiya jata hai.

Case Studies:

Case studies practical applications ko samajhne mein madad karti hain. **MYCIN** ek case study hai, jo medical diagnosis ke liye ek successful expert system tha.

Learning Methods:

AI mein **learning** se system apni knowledge improve karta hai. **Rote Learning, Inductive Learning**, aur **Explanation-Based Learning** yeh teen main techniques hain, jo expert systems mein use hoti hain.

- **Rote Learning** mein system simply facts ya examples yaad karta hai.

- **Inductive Learning** mein system specific examples se rules ya patterns seekhta hai.

- **Explanation-Based Learning** mein system apne decisions ko analyze karta hai aur uss analysis se apni decision-making improve karta hai.